OUT OF THIS WORLD

Beyond Imagination

Edited By Georgia Osborne

First published in Great Britain in 2020 by:

Young Writers
Remus House
Coltsfoot Drive
Peterborough
PE2 9BF
Telephone: 01733 890066
Website: www.youngwriters.co.uk

All Rights Reserved
Book Design by Ashley Janson
© Copyright Contributors 2020
Softback ISBN 978-1-83928-903-3

Printed and bound in the UK by BookPrintingUK
Website: www.bookprintinguk.com
YB0441B

FOREWORD

Here at Young Writers our defining aim is to promote the joys of reading and writing to children and young adults and we are committed to nurturing the creative talents of the next generation. By allowing them to see their own work in print we believe their confidence and love of creative writing will grow.

Out Of This World is our latest fantastic competition, specifically designed to encourage the writing skills of primary school children through the medium of poetry. From the high quality of entries received, it is clear that it really captured the imagination of all involved.

We are proud to present the resulting collection of poems that we are sure will amuse and inspire.

An absorbing insight into the imagination and thoughts of the young, we hope you will agree that this fantastic anthology is one to delight the whole family again and again.

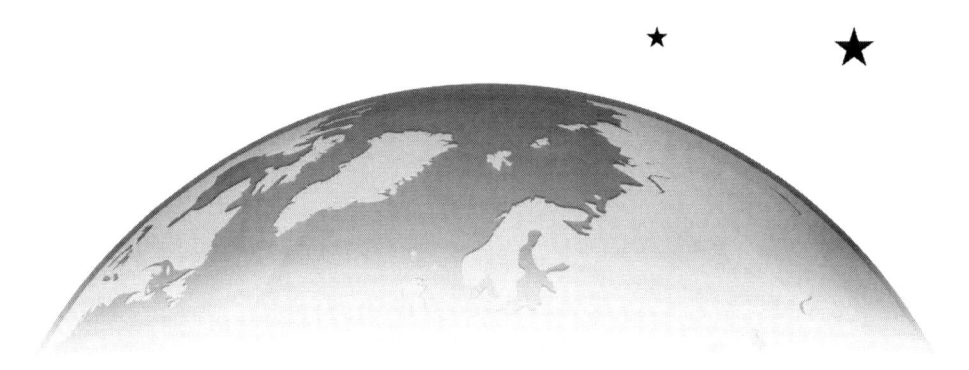

CONTENTS

Bruton Primary School, Bruton

Brandon (11)	1
Laila Laurie (11)	2
Holly (11)	4
Rosie (10)	5
Nell Farquhar (11)	6
Anna (10)	8
Isaac Crossman (11)	9
Iyla (10)	10
Layla Hole (10)	11
Lucy Wilcox (10)	12
Henry Shepherd	13
Archie Stokes (10)	14
Tom Runacre (11)	15
Dexter (10)	16
Lily (10)	17
Toby Meadowcroft (11)	18
Josh Adams (11)	19
Oliver (10)	20
Imogen Madge (11)	21
Sunny (10)	22
Jack (11)	23
George Ashford-Dargie (10)	24
Mackenzie (11)	25

Charlesworth Primary School, Charlesworth

Mallory Dowson (7)	26
Abigail Feehily (9)	27
Lottie Charlton (7)	28
Hugo Crowton (8)	29
George Turley (9)	30
Seth Pryce (8)	31
Harry Dean (7)	32

Órla McHale (8)	33
Harry Turley (7)	34
Ben Barton (7)	35
Jayden Guttridge (7)	36
Alfie Metcalf (8)	37
Kaiden Collier (9)	38
Bram Milne (9)	39
Bethany Roden (8)	40
Ellie-Jayne Summersgill (7)	41
Riley Choppin (7)	42

Harris Primary Academy Philip Lane, Tottenham

Takiyah Angelique Leon (11)	43
Amina Povacaj (10)	44
Ariana Melnychull (10)	46
Lily Thompson (10)	47
Abdoul Sayari (10)	48

Regius School, Newcraighall

Joseph Vogan (10)	49
Ewan Phillipson (11)	50
Zoe Mayer (9)	51
Maria Kluszewska (11)	52
Brendan Stewart (11)	53
Sanna Stewart (9)	54
Jason Abban (10)	55
Jean Dalo (10)	56
Chantae Anderson (10)	57
Elia Powell (9)	58
Hania Kluszewska (9)	59

St Benedict's Catholic Primary School, Warrington

Lily Kane (8)	60
Ronnie Hutchinson (9)	61
Jack McGee (9)	62
Lily-Mai Louise Naylor (9)	63
Jakub Kluzek (9)	64
Jennifer Diamond (8)	65
Isobelle Holden (8)	66
Csenge Puskas (9)	67
Lola Lawton (8)	68
Lily Mai Cavanagh (8)	69
Charlie Bennett (9)	70
Ashton Myers (8)	71
Lily McDermott (8)	72
Violet Tinker (8)	73
Maisy Powell (9)	74
Hope Doherty (8)	75
Megan Malone (9)	76
Grace Forde (9)	77
Erin Forrest (8)	78
Drey Tee (9)	79

St Mary's Catholic Primary School, Fleetwood

Lucas Randles (11)	80
Declan Whiteside (11)	82
Bradley Swain (11)	84
Beau Mckenna (11)	86
Kane Jones (10)	88
Natalie Roberts (10)	90
Jack Griffin (10)	92
Dzhuliya Hristova (10)	94
Ben Mellow (10)	96
Siyana Angelova (9)	98
Alex Gawne (11)	100
Brooke Whittaker (9)	102
Blossom Martinez (10)	104
Alfie Southern (10)	106
Demi-Doll Broughan (10)	107

Werrington Primary School, Werrington

Molly Francis (10)	108
Kendal Gallacher (9)	109
James Sherratt (9)	110
Miley Woodhouse (9)	111
Marshall Miller (10)	112
Chloe Longton (9)	113
Sydney Shaw (10)	114
George Mayer (10)	115
Eden Leigh (9)	116
Danielle Cunningham (10)	117
Kadem Mayer (10)	118
Saphron Love (9)	119
Samuel Ledgar (10)	120
Maisy Jackson (10)	121
Ollie McDonnell (9)	122
Logan Parker Nixon (9)	123
Chloe McLoughlin (10)	124
Megan Plant (10)	125
Daniel Summerfield (10)	126
Flo Sawyer (10)	127
Charlie Kemp (9)	128
Isla Salt (10)	129
Daniella Owen (9)	130
Lola Stevens (10)	131
Isla Talbot (9)	132
Maizey Statham (10)	133
Hope Clulow (10)	134
Charlie Edwards (10)	135
Elliot Pass (9)	136
Violet Parton (9)	137
Millie McGill (9)	138
Lucas Baskeyfield (10)	139
Millie Bowker (10)	140
Noah Haddon (10)	141
Jacob Leach (10)	142
Oliver Degg (10)	143
Isabelle Pennington (9)	144
Reuben Donnellan (10)	145
Isaac Williams (9)	146
Sam Trowell (10)	147
Maddie Prince	148

Ryan Wright (9) 149
Olivia Edge (9) 150
Grace Gilbert (9) 151
Oliver Jackson (10) 152
Layton Mottram (10) 153

West Walton Community Primary School, West Walton

Maddie Byron (10) 154
Macie Anne Maplesden (10) 156
Ellie Cavill (11) 157
Maison Rider (10) 158
Megan Slack (11) 159
Lyndon Barton (11) 160
Arthur Buckler (10) 161
Gracie Jane Walker (10) 162
Simona Bislyte (11) 163
Norvile Petrilovskyte (10) 164
Samantha Blyth (10) 165
Ben Notley (10) 166
Lucy Mae McClure (10) 167

Wood Farm Primary School, Headington

Kacper Jakub Mackowski (9) 168
Rukhsora Imamnazarova (11) 169
Lucas Brooks (9) 170
Klaudia Stawinska (9) 172
Grace Champion (9) 173
Ayman Saadi Mahir (9) 174
Hamdi Guled Hasan (10) 175
Liana Roopesh (10) 176
Stephana Sojan (9) 177
Inaaya Bibi Asghar (11) 178
Daniella Drizi (9) 179
Adina Nadeem-Aftab (10) 180
Manroop Singh (10) 181
Senara Bambaravanage (11) 182
Hadia Haydari (10) 183
Harry Stillman 184
Almuez Amier Alagab (11) 185

THE POEMS

The Black Panther

Hiding in the trees, waiting for its prey,
When the moment comes it pounces.
Back in the trees, camouflaged with its black skin,
Its white sharp teeth bite strong like a big T-rex.

If the prey gets away,
The mightly beast will let its speed go wild.
If you are the prey then I would stay away,
Because the mighty predator is the black panther.

Bones scattered around from its big prey,
It's not hungry anymore because of its feast.
Black panther, black panther, hiding in the trees,
Predator of all the prey, the king of them all.

They hunt at night and sleep in the day,
Black panthers will take you down with no regrets.

Brandon (11)
Bruton Primary School, Bruton

A Spider Monkey's Dream

I live in the jungle;
I love to play.
My home is hot,
But sometimes my tail gets wet.
When this happens
I simply moan and whine,
And Mum tells me I'm not brave.
But I know she's just the same.

I love to eat,
I love to jump,
But the older boys are scary and tough.
Their noses are wider,
They have longer legs,
I feel scared,
But not for long,
As my best friend appears.

As graceful as a gliding hawk,
And with the beauty of a thousand swans,

They stumble and fall
Down to the jungle floor.

The fur on my back may still be fluffy,
But I know,
I will save my country,
I will be a Super Spider Monkey.

I know this won't happen until I'm three,
But I hope this dream will fulfil me.

Laila Laurie (11)
Bruton Primary School, Bruton

The Octopus

He has deep black eyes like the bottom of the ocean;
A big floppy head like jelly on a plate;
Wriggly legs that curl at the ends,
He scuttles along the seafloor,
Looking for a feast to gobble up with his razor-sharp beak.

He has suction cups underneath him
Like a child's toothbrush stuck to the sink,
Camouflaged against the ocean floor,
Inking his predators then hurrying away.

He is an escape artist,
He can get through any gap,
Slithering and squeezing through any obstacle
That comes in his way.

He hides in crevices,
Feeling the tide pull,
Watching the water darken
Hour by hour.

Holly (11)
Bruton Primary School, Bruton

Mr Octopus

Mr Octopus:
One of the smartest animals I know,
I've never met any of your aunts or uncles,
You live down in the ocean, far too low.

If I were to see you,
You would know what I think,
A human in my world,
You'd splash me with ink.

You're very flexible,
I've heard you could fit in a tiny jar,
You're also very smart,
If you tried, you could probably drive a car.

Your tentacles suck on so tight,
But are as wobbly as jelly.
You have a beak for a mouth,
And I've always wondered, where's your belly?

Rosie (10)
Bruton Primary School, Bruton

Scops

Eyes,
Staring malevolently out of the feathers,
The peepers I owe so much to.
Round as beach balls,
Orange as tangerines,
Eyes.

Feathers,
Dashed and streaked with black,
A grey rock hunched on the sand.
Minute as eyelashes,
Delicate as lace,
Feathers.

Beak,
Poking out of the moustache-like crines,
A tough, insect-eating hook of iron.
Quick as lightning,
Keen as an arrow,
Beak.

Feet,
As strong and supple as snakes,
And armed with talons as cruel as knives.
Gnarly as tree trunks,
Sharp as a ferret's bite,
Feet.

Nell Farquhar (11)
Bruton Primary School, Bruton

The Cute Black Shetland Pony

This is my shetland pony.
My shetland pony is dark and shiny black,
As shiny as glass polished bright,
Just a day ago.
His mane is long and silky,
And very well brushed.
His tail the same,
Just very long,
And touches the floor,
When he begins to trot.
This is my shetland pony, my shetland pony,
Can trot like a stallion in pride,
And walk calmly by your side.
He stands there like a lamppost,
Waiting for his energy to come back to him.
My shetland loves to run,
He runs around like mad,
And loves to have some fun.

Anna (10)
Bruton Primary School, Bruton

Guilty Gators

I am a gator, as tough as can be,
I'm not that fun when I'm hungry,
So don't taunt me.
My teeth are as sharp as a machete,
And my scales are rougher than the sea.

My eyes are as sharp as a razor blade,
So don't taunt me.
I can camouflage in the water,
You won't notice me.

I might be bigger than a croc,
But I don't hurt any more than they do.
Sometimes it can get a bit lonely,
So that's a reason I can get angry,
So do not taunt me.

Isaac Crossman (11)
Bruton Primary School, Bruton

Octopus

Hypnotising colours
Like an illusion in a science lab.
Hearts (there are three) the size of tennis balls.
There are similarities, but yet there are differences.
It lives in the deep, right at the bottom,
His mouth is at the other end.
There are similarities, but yet there are differences.
Jelly-like body, it's truly fantastic.
He has legs like slimy, stretchy, elastic.
There are similarities, but there are differences.
There are similarities, but yet there are differences.

Iyla (10)
Bruton Primary School, Bruton

The Snow Lynx

Its claws and teeth are like razor blades.
Its feet are larger than its fluffy body.
The white fur lets it camouflage in the snow when hunting.
The white, thick snow gives it great camouflage
For a stealth-like mission.
If in a bush, the spots are like berries,
So prey comes to eat them,
But the lynx gets there first,
Springing high as it runs like a kangaroo.
Its large, furry feet help it move easily on the snow.
The fur coat helps keep it warm, to snuggle with her cubs.

Layla Hole (10)
Bruton Primary School, Bruton

Parrots

Parrots fly through the trees,
Squawking their heads off.
Colours look pretty like the sun and the sea,
Massive birds in the jungle.
Claws are sharp like knives,
Good at perching on logs.
Lives in the jungles of South America,
Curved beaks help them eat,
They fight to mate.

They fly hundreds of miles around the forest,
Meeting other parrots on the way,
Small and big parrots,
Babies are so cute.

You must take care of parrots.

Lucy Wilcox (10)
Bruton Primary School, Bruton

The Spider

Eyes as sharp as daggers
Glinting in the sun,
Legs are scary for everyone.

People look at me
Like a monster,
And I don't know why,
When I help get rid of a fly.

I run as fast as a cheetah,
Thanks to my eight legs;
They are as grippy as eight pegs.

My thoughts about life are quite sure,
And it's funny how they occur.

You're afraid of me and I'm afraid of you,
Some people flush me down the loo!

Henry Shepherd
Bruton Primary School, Bruton

The Royal Python

I'm a royal python,
I won't harm you.
Leave me alone please,
Can you leave me to my own business?

I might scare you,
You don't want to know,
My eyes are like crackling flames burning,
They're like two daggers glinting in the sun.

I slither, not slimy, into the lapping waves,
Through the rainforests I go.
I mark my territory in African rainforests.
My colours are multiple and all have patterns.

Archie Stokes (10)
Bruton Primary School, Bruton

Exquisite Elephants

With stomping feet,
As hard as a rock.
Clear white tusks,
As strong as metal.
A majestic trunk,
Waving in the wind.

Floppy ears,
Like a velvet blanket.
A thousand wrinkles,
On each bit of its body.
Withered eyes,
With a bold, brown glint.

I might move slow,
But I'm very strong.
I'm super protective,
Over my young.
I walk in herds,
I am the matriarch.

Tom Runacre (11)
Bruton Primary School, Bruton

The Cheetah

My fur is yellow with black spots,
I'm strolling through the African plains,
Looking for my dinner.
I have spotted a gazelle,
Not that far away;
I'm sneaking up behind it,
Stealthy as a snake,
And I pounce on it,
And I bite it,
And I scratch it,
And it's down on the ground.
I munch on it like I haven't eaten in months,
And I finish it up,
And that's my evening.

Dexter (10)
Bruton Primary School, Bruton

The Piggies

Hiding in their round metal homes,
Filled with straw,
All cute and snuggly,
Waiting to be born.

Staring at the starry sky,
Wanting to be loved,
All cute and fluffy,
Snuffling around.

Some are big,
Some are small,
Just like us.

Pigs don't catch other animals,
Instead, they just eat mud.
They don't want to get involved,
Just doing their own stuff.

Lily (10)
Bruton Primary School, Bruton

The King Of The Cobras

My teeth as sharp as a rhino's horn,
Venom more deadly than a spider,
And eyes of an evil lord.
I slither like slime,
I'll bite if I have to,
And inject doom deep.
People charm me out of a basket,
Only if I let them.

I'm as fast as a cheetah,
Slick as a fox,
My name is cool,
That's why I'm the king of
The cobras!

Toby Meadowcroft (11)
Bruton Primary School, Bruton

The Not A Crab Crab

I'm a horseshoe crab,
I am not hostile,
I wish you no harm,
Just leave me alone,
And leave me to be calm.

Do not be scared,
I am quite friendly,
Just leave me alone,
And my tail will not harm you.

I'm nature's tank,
Bronze like a penny,
Almost bulletproof,
And I slide like a hockey puck on ice.

Josh Adams (11)
Bruton Primary School, Bruton

The Frog

The frog's eyes are as orange as a crackling fire,
Pupils as sharp as a needle,
Catching flies on the top of a tongue,
With the colours of a leaf on a winter's day, as wet as can be.
Tongue as sticky as a tangerine,
I wish I could be so green,
Leaping from leaf to leaf,
Croaking like a cricket.

Oliver (10)
Bruton Primary School, Bruton

The Peacock

Its body is a sapphire blue,
Shaped like an hourglass,
It has a long beak,
And its pupils are as black as coal.

Its feathers make him look like someone from a carnival,
With a million eyes looking at you.
Its colours are taken from an ocean palette,
And it's very intimidating.

Imogen Madge (11)
Bruton Primary School, Bruton

My Little Pink Piglet

My little pink piglet is as bright as my new jumper,
Getting muddy in her brown home.

Snorting to get my attention,
Clever little piglet.

Just remember she's mine, not yours.
When she is big,
And has piglets of her own,
I will still call her my little pink piglet.

Sunny (10)
Bruton Primary School, Bruton

The Sturgeon

The sturgeon, as deadly as a great white shark
Leans out of the river,
Guarding its territory.
Sixty-five million years ago,
The sturgeon is back there,
And now it's nearly extinct!

Jack (11)
Bruton Primary School, Bruton

Rattlesnake

Its eyes as hypnotising as chocolate,
But not creamy, not tough, or smooth.
With scales as smooth as butter,
But as hard as earth.
As speedy as an arrow.
Slithery as squid legs squirm.

George Ashford-Dargie (10)
Bruton Primary School, Bruton

Lamb

My lamb is as fluffy as candyfloss,
As white as clouds.
My lamb is as cute as a little dog,
As cool as a celebrity.

Mackenzie (11)
Bruton Primary School, Bruton

Pyramid

P yramids are as pointy as the bottom of an ice cream cone.
Y ellow sand feels like you are on the beach.
R ows of plants by the river Nile.
A ncient Egypt has a lot of pyramids.
M ysterious pyramids are full of secrets.
I n the pyramids are secrets.
D on't climb to the top of a pyramid!

Mallory Dowson (7)
Charlesworth Primary School, Charlesworth

Pyramid

P haraohs in tombs.
Y ellow, sandy, and dry like sand.
R eally hot inside there, and gloomy.
A mazingly taller than any house ever made.
M assive and very sandy, also really high.
I mportant to many people who live in Egypt.
D angerous to climb because you could fall.

Abigail Feehily (9)
Charlesworth Primary School, Charlesworth

Pyramid

P yramids are as pointy as cats' ears.
Y ellow bricks stacked on top of each other.
R eally pointy pyramids.
A ncient treasures belong to rich pharaohs.
M ysterious ancient pyramids.
I ncredible old pyramids.
D isgracefully golden and shiny.

Lottie Charlton (7)
Charlesworth Primary School, Charlesworth

Pyramid

P ointy as a thorn.
Y ellow like the extremely hot sun.
R eally old, sturdy pyramids.
A mazing, extraordinary secrets.
M ajestic, mirroring, shiny gold.
I ncredibly ancient mummies.
D isplays his royal history inside.

Hugo Crowton (8)
Charlesworth Primary School, Charlesworth

Pyramid Poem

P ointy as a beak.
Y ellow as the sun.
R uined buildings with dead people inside.
A mazing features that wait inside.
M ummies come out to terrorise.
I f I was a mummy, what would I do,
D ead in a very small tube?

George Turley (9)
Charlesworth Primary School, Charlesworth

Ancient Egypt

P ale.
Y oung? No.
R eally beautiful.
A mazing artefacts.
M ysterious, amazing facts inside.
I definitely want to find out more.
D esperate to dig out Tutankhamun's death mask.

Seth Pryce (8)
Charlesworth Primary School, Charlesworth

Pyramid Poem

P ointed like the top of Big Ben.
Y ellow like a lemon.
R ich pharaohs live in them.
A ncient and old.
M ummies are put in them.
I gloos are smaller than them.
D anger: Keep out!

Harry Dean (7)
Charlesworth Primary School, Charlesworth

Pyramid

P recious and pointy.
Y ellow and sandy like the sun.
R uined and extraordinary.
A n ancient tomb of pharaohs.
M assive.
I 'm as small as a leaf.
D anger, blinding pyramids!

Órla McHale (8)
Charlesworth Primary School, Charlesworth

Pyramid

P haraohs are in pyramids.
Y ellow sandstone pyramids.
R usty stone pyramids.
A ncient pyramids.
M ysterious hidden secrets.
I ncredible ancient secrets.
D ark, magical history.

Harry Turley (7)
Charlesworth Primary School, Charlesworth

Ancient Egypt Pyramid Poem

P haraoh.
Y ellowy gold.
R uined and destroyed.
A s big as a mountain.
M ummies are buried there.
I dare you to climb to the top.
D anger: Do not enter! Danger: Do not enter!

Ben Barton (7)
Charlesworth Primary School, Charlesworth

Pyramid

P ointy pyramids.
Y ellow as the hot sun.
R uined home.
A ncient Egypt.
M ysterious homes.
I feel as small as a mouse.
D usty things.
S hiny taps.

Jayden Guttridge (7)
Charlesworth Primary School, Charlesworth

Pyramid

P haraohs.
Y ellow, glimmering sun.
R ed Sea protects everyone in Egypt.
A ncient Egypt.
M ysterious Underworld.
I ncredible pyramids.
D azzling sand.

Alfie Metcalf (8)
Charlesworth Primary School, Charlesworth

Pyramid

P haraohs.
Y ellow, light sand.
R uined bricks.
A s hot as the sun.
M any pyramids have pharaohs.
I feel scared.
D anger: Don't go further.

Kaiden Collier (9)
Charlesworth Primary School, Charlesworth

Pyramid

P yramid.
Y ellow like a banana.
R uined, smashed bricks.
A mazing and massive.
M agic, mysterious.
I feel like an insect.
D iamonds inside.

Bram Milne (9)
Charlesworth Primary School, Charlesworth

Pyramid

P ointy and precious.
Y ellow like a lemon.
R uined.
A ncient.
M ysterious.
I 'm as small as a leaf.
D angerous like Mount Everest.

Bethany Roden (8)
Charlesworth Primary School, Charlesworth

Pyramid

P ointy.
Y ellow, dusty pyramids.
R usty, sandy bricks.
A ncient Egypt.
M ystical, spooky.
I ncredible.
D ead-black pyramid.

Ellie-Jayne Summersgill (7)
Charlesworth Primary School, Charlesworth

Pyramid

P ointy pyramid.
Y ellow sun.
R eally old.
A ncient Egypt.
M ummies.
I n the pyramids are secrets.
D eath of the kings.

Riley Choppin (7)
Charlesworth Primary School, Charlesworth

Alien Girl

An alien had landed on a weird planet, so she looked around. Her name is Rosie. She has lilac, fair skin and two little horns. Rosie has black eyes, long, flowing, glossy red hair, with coloured flowers. She wears a short dress with a golden, shiny belt and comfy shoes.

A lovely girl helped Rosie with her mum and gave her some food. She slept in a bed in the little girl's room and built a ship.

It was time to go, Rosie went to say goodbye to the family. She got in the ship and flew to her planet. All her friends missed her, Rosie missed her dog as well and went to her house. She told them about the majestic family and went to see them again. The girl was surprised and hugged Rosie very tight. Her friends loved them too.

Takiyah Angelique Leon (11)
Harris Primary Academy Philip Lane, Tottenham

Save Our Planet

We are all selfish murderers,
Killing the reason we are alive,
Destroying it slowly
By thrashing it with trash
That are like knives.

Help the whale!
Please don't step on that poor snail!
I'm sure it's just started its proper life.

Leave the poor forests alone!
Don't you dare burn them down like coal.
Save endangered species,
They won't be here for long.

We are changing how fish migrate,
Causing coral reefs to die.
Australia is flooding,
The poor trees are burning.
Koalas are trying to escape,
But they aren't having much faith.

The endangered species are now 41,415.
So please save our beautiful Earth!

Amina Povacaj (10)
Harris Primary Academy Philip Lane, Tottenham

Shooting Stars

Bright like stars,
But even brighter,
Near Mars.
Even nicer,
Than a piece of glass,
I wonder what it is
A star? Probably not.
In my head a song pops up,
'Shine bright like a diamond!'
OMG is it a diamond?
Oh, never mind!
Wait, it's moving...
A shooting star.
She made a wish and it came true,
It was the best day of her life.

Ariana Melnychull (10)
Harris Primary Academy Philip Lane, Tottenham

To Saturn

I am going on a little trip,
To Saturn on my rocket ship.
What to bring, I can't decide,
My teddy bear or mouse called Clyde?
Or maybe even my dragon called Smiffy,
I told him we'd be there in a jiffy.
He said no so we had to go
To get the marshmallow
For me and Clyde to eat along the way
Until we get to Saturn!

Lily Thompson (10)
Harris Primary Academy Philip Lane, Tottenham

Demonic Dragon

There's a dragon in space,
Who eats his prey in a race,
Who jumps from planet to planet,
Just like a rabbit.

His feet are gargantuan and wide,
His camouflaging body helps him in space,
To cheat in every race.

This monstrous creature,
Will only be a teacher,
Of cheating.

Abdoul Sayari (10)
Harris Primary Academy Philip Lane, Tottenham

What Am I?

A sailor's tale, a Greek myth,
Impossible trail, ship strayed,
Captain dismayed, eating some god's cattle.
Hairbrained soldiers did the deed,
Taken by hunger, cries in battle
Vs Poseidon, they couldn't be stronger,
But the brain is better than the possession
Of the Pacific. Old sea-faring Cap',
Wasn't daring to use a map,
When facing a whirlpool and
A six-headed monster twice,
As well as going into the land
Of the dead. Didn't bat an eyelid
At the ghosts disappearing without a trace
Or when the sirens confused his head.
One of the best books I've read,
What am I?

I am The Odyssey.

Joseph Vogan (10)
Regius School, Newcraighall

A Man Called Lee

There once was a man called Lee
Who wanted to learn to ski.
He went up a mountain,
Fell into a fountain,
Then went down saying, "I am Speed!"

He went up the mountain again.
Then it started to pour with rain.
He slid on his bum,
So he had some rum,
Then he fell when it reached his brain.

He woke wrapped up in some blankets,
With a plate full of large crumpets,
He saw his best dog,
He thought he saw God,
Then he realised he's on antibiotics!

Ewan Phillipson (11)
Regius School, Newcraighall

Wild Animals!

There once was a lovely wild hare.
His favourite fruit was pear,
He ate only that!
So one day, a cat
Came and ate up all the pear!

There once was a nice, kind fox,
Who got stuck inside a small box.
He shouted for help
And gave a loud yelp,
But he was still stuck in the box!

There once was a lovely red deer,
Who only had one right ear.
She ran every day
In the woods every way,
But she still only had one ear.

Zoe Mayer (9)
Regius School, Newcraighall

The Earth

The Earth is dying and so are we.
Fires are spreading and no one is helping.
Australia is burning, and also it flooded.
Climate change is getting worse.
Pandas and sea turtles are nearly extinct.

We humans have to step it up.
We have to stop and realise what we're doing.
We have to stop putting trash everywhere,
And start really thinking about our world.
Think of the damage we are giving our Earth.

Maria Kluszewska (11)
Regius School, Newcraighall

Dragons

Dragons breathe their fire,
Their bodies hard as steel.
If they could live on Earth,
They would be a big deal.

Not to kill them, not to shoot.
Not to hunt them or to put
Any types of traps and gigs
Just for all the loot.

All is the darkness
At night where people rest.
Here comes the dragon
That has its flaming chest.

Brendan Stewart (11)
Regius School, Newcraighall

Our Best Friend!

Dogs are so faithful.
Dogs are so energetic.
Puppies are so wild.

Cats are companions.
Cats are so cute when they play,
But sometimes crazy!

Rabbits are restful.
Rabbits eat a lot of carrots.
They don't mess around!

Pets are so loyal.
Pets are so obedient.
They are our best friends!

Sanna Stewart (9)
Regius School, Newcraighall

The Body

Your body is a great machine,
You need to keep your body clean,
Venom will not stay
Because it's decay.
Your body is a great machine.

Your body is a great machine,
It's the best robot I've ever seen,
It's the healthiest,
And the stealthiest.
It's the best machine ever seen.

Jason Abban (10)
Regius School, Newcraighall

The Bee And Pete

There was a bee with tiny feet,
Who was so keen to go and meet,
How can I not bear
To meet this new heir
When going to greet the Queen?

The small bee came with Tiny Pete.
Tiny Pete was ever so mean,
He could not bear
To lose his own friend.
There were two small bees with tiny feet.

Jean Dalo (10)
Regius School, Newcraighall

The Dog In The Shoe

There once was a little puppy
And its name was little Luppy.
He got stuck in a shoe
And he needed the loo.
There once was a little puppy.

There once was a big, fluffy dog
And its name was big old Ogg.
He wanted to bark
To a little lark.
There once was a big, fluffy dog.

Chantae Anderson (10)
Regius School, Newcraighall

Sweet Sunny Spring

S pring is beautiful.
P eople love going out into the sun.
R oses grow and are beautiful.
I n spring deer run about in the fresh air.
N ormally it's warm but sometimes cold.
G rass is fresh green and the trees are beautiful.

Elia Powell (9)
Regius School, Newcraighall

What Am I?

I'm as orange as the sun.
My leaves are as rich as gold.
I'm here right now, but soon I'll be gone.
What am I?

I am autumn leaves.

Hania Kluszewska (9)
Regius School, Newcraighall

Shooting Star

S oaring through the sky like a butterfly,
H urtling through space, it's got so much grace.
O bviously, I am scared, just like a scary bear.
O ut of this Earth, there's an alien.
T urning our heads so we can see outside,
I t's going to be a fantastic night.
N ever going to have a better experience in my life.
G etting out of the rocket so we can see the stars flying past me, it's going to be an awesome ride.

S aving the planet that night,
T aking out the costume of an astronaut, I'm finally alike.
A wesome, I wished a wish upon a star
R acing in the air like a flying kid's nightmare.

Lily Kane (8)
St Benedict's Catholic Primary School, Warrington

Shooting Star

S licing through the cold, windy air,
H ear the twinkles from the sky,
O ver the Earth, having fun,
O uter space is darker than a cave,
T he sight of it is getting smaller, smaller, and smaller,
I n the sky, aliens say hello,
N ight-time comes with a special surprise for every alien.
G liding through the sky the aliens wave goodbye.

S hooting stars are amazing,
T he sound of it was beautiful,
A time for celebration,
R ight, it's time to go to sleep.

Ronnie Hutchinson (9)
St Benedict's Catholic Primary School, Warrington

Shooting Star

S upernatural visitors came round for tea, also to say hi.
H e's just nipping by,
O r he's just coming with his kids.
O ut of this world! He's not named Sid!
T he amazing wonders,
I 've always started to ponder
N othing ever gets better.
G o, I'm putting on my space sweater.

S uch an amazing sight.
T he things, so bright,
A s amazing as a chameleon
R acing through the stars as bright as neon.

Jack McGee (9)
St Benedict's Catholic Primary School, Warrington

Shooting Star

S hooting star racing across Earth,
H ave you ever seen a shooting star?
O h, closing our eyes and praying,
O ur dreams will come true.
T he star is glittering in the sky.
I can see the shooting star glittering in the sky!
N ever have I seen a shooting star before
G littering in the sky.

S topping and watching the shooting star,
T he stars are beautiful,
A re flashing like a car,
R acing like lightning.

Lily-Mai Louise Naylor (9)
St Benedict's Catholic Primary School, Warrington

Shooting Star

S uper fast and natural visitor,
H oping to see one and make a wish!
O uter space all around it,
O ozing down the huge outer space.
T he shooting star is across Belgium,
I n the sky, it looks like a marble.
N ever seen, or can be seen,
G etting ready to go away.

S eeping through the world granting wishes,
T he shooting star is as fast as Concord.
A beautiful sight,
R acing endlessly over the stars.

Jakub Kluzek (9)
St Benedict's Catholic Primary School, Warrington

Flying Star

S hining brightly,
H owling every day,
O ver there is where it goes
O ver the mountains, it roams.
T en miles an hour it goes,
I 've never seen anything like it before.
N ever to be seen again,
G oing so fast you only see a flash.

S creaming excitedly,
T en miles it has covered today.
A fter an hour it is gone,
R acing through the sky.

Jennifer Diamond (8)
St Benedict's Catholic Primary School, Warrington

The Shooting Star

S himmering through the sky,
H overing through the air,
O ver in the air, round, round and round.
O ut of this world.
T hinking what might happen next,
I n and out through the stars,
N othing bothering it.
G ranting wishes,

S hining through the midnight sky,
T aking its time,
A rriving on Earth,
R eady to go!

Isobelle Holden (8)
St Benedict's Catholic Primary School, Warrington

Shooting Star

S hining brighter than the sun,
H eating up high in the sky,
O ur bodies in shakes,
O ut in the sky,
T urning our heads to the sky,
I n the sky up high,
N earer and nearer to the sky,
G oing up in the sky, up high.

S aying hi and bye,
T earing out of sight,
A re our eyes sparkling bright,
R oaring in the sky.

Csenge Puskas (9)
St Benedict's Catholic Primary School, Warrington

Out Of This World!

S hinning like a diamond,
H owling through the air,
O ur supernatural visitor,
O ut of this world.
T he night sky glistening with stars,
I nviting the excitement.
N ow it's time to make a wish,
G reat like stars!

S uper like Superman!
T he party is here,
A mazingly fast,
R ushing down to Earth!

Lola Lawton (8)
St Benedict's Catholic Primary School, Warrington

Magnificent Rocket

R acing through the midnight sky, where no one would ever see,
O ver the glittery moon, astronauts would have jelly teeth,
C hattering teeth going over the Blackpool Tower.
K ids looking up in the air,
E veryone cheering,
T aking off in three, two, one... Blast-off!

Lily Mai Cavanagh (8)
St Benedict's Catholic Primary School, Warrington

The Rocket

R oaring through the sky like a lion,
O ur bodies shaking with fear,
C hattering teeth with fright,
K icking up off the stand like a cheetah,
E ven though it's twenty-nine metres high,
T hrusts bursting out with fire.

Charlie Bennett (9)
St Benedict's Catholic Primary School, Warrington

Rocket

R acing through the sky,
O ur bodies are shaking with fear,
C hattering teeth while moving everywhere.
K icks through the sky,
E ven though it was already clear.
T aking off in four, three, two, one... Blast-off!

Ashton Myers (8)
St Benedict's Catholic Primary School, Warrington

The Rocket

R eady for a flight adventure,
O ver the midnight air,
C rossing the world, here and there,
K nowing the spaceship is red,
E ven though I know we're
T aking off in a red, racing rocket!

Lily McDermott (8)
St Benedict's Catholic Primary School, Warrington

Rocket

R unning through the midnight sky,
O ver the mighty Earth below,
C hattering teeth through fear,
K icking up in the sky.
E veryone feeling good,
T omorrow it will land with a big crash!

Violet Tinker (8)
St Benedict's Catholic Primary School, Warrington

The Rocket

R acing off into the air,
O ur hands holding on tight,
C oming over the Earth,
K icking off up, up and away!
E ven though it's very heavy,
T he nerves go away as we go out of sight!

Maisy Powell (9)
St Benedict's Catholic Primary School, Warrington

The Rocket

R aging like fire through the sky,
O ur amazing ship going so high.
C olossal machine slowly disappearing,
K icks up and is not leaving.
E veryone is shouting,
T he rocket is now gone!

Hope Doherty (8)
St Benedict's Catholic Primary School, Warrington

The Rocket

R acing like a race car,
O ur bodies shaking like a balloon in the wind,
C alling goodbye,
K icking up in the air,
E ven bigger than a plane.
T aking off, three, two, one... Blast-off!

Megan Malone (9)
St Benedict's Catholic Primary School, Warrington

The Rocket

R acing through the sky,
O ver the moon, it will never die,
C ooler than ice,
K icks up like a football in the sky,
E verlasting and going high,
T he rocket has finally landed.

Grace Forde (9)
St Benedict's Catholic Primary School, Warrington

The Rocket

R eady to take off
O r already gliding through the sky,
C an you see it?
K ids screaming and chanting,
E very space invention being seen,
T rying to hear the crowd being quiet.

Erin Forrest (8)
St Benedict's Catholic Primary School, Warrington

The Rocket

R acing through the night sky,
O ver the moon,
C hattering teeth of fear,
K icks through the clouds.
E veryone cheers the rocket,
T o see it blast off.

Drey Tee (9)
St Benedict's Catholic Primary School, Warrington

The Incredible Hulk

The Hulk, a monstrous creature
Who has a head as large as nine footballs,
He roams the streets daily,
Just waiting for calls.

The giant of normal men changes
Into a colossal-sized dinosaur,
His only fear is his anger,
If you make him mad he will roar.

When he walks the ground shakes
Violently and buildings crack,
He will never be defeated
And always comes back.

Saving New York, that's what he does best,
Running around like he has no clue.
This is only one job that he has done,
He could do it with his crew.

This creature is one of a kind,
And if you punch him, it will hurt.

As strong as a mountain, he has lots of friends,
His world's best friend is called Kurt.

The amazing Bruce Banner
Is the dangerous Hulk,
Remember to leave this mossy-coloured man,
If he's in a sulk.

The Incredible Hulk is the most monstrous of them all,
Don't mess with him or he will throw you against a wall.
Hulk has the strength of all the world's men,
He will not be beaten, he always comes again.

The green giant runs around like he owns the streets,
He helps all the people in the world,
And is welcomed by everybody he meets!

Lucas Randles (11)
St Mary's Catholic Primary School, Fleetwood

The Prince Of Mischief!

I am Loki, the one and only,
I've got many friends, but sometimes I'm lonely.

I am powerful and childish and like to cause mischief,
Although I am full of powers, don't class me as a thief.

I can make you authentically useful,
You would not want to shoot me with a rifle.

My enemies can be seen from a lengthy distance,
Some people say I need assistance.

The emerald suit owned by Loki,
Is being worn whilst flicking a bogey.

As soon as I walk through the door,
"Let's go fight!" says my brother, Thor.

Very irritating, potential poky Loki,
Is always doing the hokey pokey.

As I was in space,
I was floating as slow as a sack race.

With my verdant cloak and piercing golden horns,
My weapons are as wounding as a million spiky thorns.

Crash! I drifted straight out of the portal hitting concrete,
People think I am a cheat.

I, Loki, am the strongest in the world,
I fight people who are hard and their body is curled.

The fight was a piece of cake,
Even though some people believe my powers are fake.

Declan Whiteside (11)
St Mary's Catholic Primary School, Fleetwood

I Am Iron Man

His most famous line "I am Iron Man,"
The glamorous armour made of steel, as hard as a can.
Line spoke in two thousand and eight,
He mainly uses helpless young lives as bait.

Saving the universe while heading to the moon,
After his near-impossible job is complete, you'll see him soon.
Great friends with the famous Captain America, also known as Steve Rogers,
But for several years, they are being immortal dodgers!

Boom! Bang! Sound covers New York as he equips his enormous laserbeam,
The main thing he does is work with a powerful team.
The one thing he fears is losing the one he dearly loves,
When he's around them, Tony is as caring as a turtle dove.

He throws his excellent equipment in anger through the walls,
But to take his anger out with his daughter, he kicks around a ball.
Tony brags on and on about how much he owns,
During the period in which the others moan.

In authentic, awesome *Endgame*, at the start, he was shaking his head,
Unsurprisingly, at the emotional end he is dead.
He must have been the richest man alive,
Except he didn't own a hive.

Bradley Swain (11)
St Mary's Catholic Primary School, Fleetwood

Hulk Does It Again

The dazzling, emerald, humungous Hulk, a car-smashing machine,
Not good in disguise, as he can easily be seen.

If you had seen this monster at night,
You would be guaranteed a fright.

The raging machine can be very vile,
But can still be a hero from a very far mile.

He started off grey, but now he is green,
It is questionable to me how he is so keen.

Boom! The strongest Avenger ever survives an explosion,
It wasn't surprising that it caused a commotion.

Wow! He has jumped up to space,
He might come flying back down so I watch out just in case.

He might not be able to die of old age,
But he will certainly kill you if you aren't on the same page.

The man has had three different mini-mes,
They all want to take the lead.

All of the villains that he quickly hopefully fights,
Have eyes brighter than Christmas lights.

Everything Hulk does is a piece of cake,
When people see him, they jump into a lake.

The dazzling, emerald, humungous Hulk, a car-smashing machine,
Not so good in disguise, as he can easily be seen.

Beau Mckenna (11)
St Mary's Catholic Primary School, Fleetwood

Spider-Man's Journey

Boom! Spider-Man has just entered the spacious room,
He was on a mission to attempt to swing to the charcoal, cosmic moon.

With determination, he tries and tries again,
He has an extremely large brain.

His secret identity is Parker, we know him as Spider-Man,
He courageously fights for justice, does whatever a spider can.

As a small boy, he loved doing science,
Now he fights vicious, vile villains, with his defiance.

Speedily, he comes up with a phenomenal plan,
While the Hulk is standing over ten feet taller than the average man.

With agility, he'll swing, swing, swing,
Through the peaceful sky whilst the bells ring.

When he's afraid, he's wearing his red and blue mask,
He always successfully finishes his task.

He has black menacing pincers and silky white webs as sticky as honey,
Spider-Man battles in all weather, though he likes it sunny.

He'll be back soon, as quick as a flash,
From capturing villains, he will dash.

Kane Jones (10)
St Mary's Catholic Primary School, Fleetwood

The Master Of Mystic Arts

Whilst walking into the disastrous town,
The towering crumbled buildings are starting to fall down.

My hands are shaking like maracas being played,
But my astronomical powers will never fade.

Looking ahead into the gloomy, misty distance,
I could see the evil villains with their powers of resistance.

Boom! As another shoots down at the ground,
Making a hole in the floor which is deep and round.

I'm defiant and determined to save New York,
But it's hard to save lives when you can hardly walk.

People were looking at me like it was a piece of cake,
But I tell you, those people don't know how much villains take.

Stones and rocks are falling like lightning,
If you were stood in my shoes, it's extremely frightening.

My ruby red cape is flying like a seagull in the wind,
Whilst I'm walking to the villains who have badly sinned.

My strong, serpent spells are shooting out my hands,
As I, Doctor Strange, will save my land.

Natalie Roberts (10)
St Mary's Catholic Primary School, Fleetwood

Wonder Woman

Legend has it, she's made from clay,
Defeating villains all day.

Armed with a lasso of truth and a magic crown,
She will always be able to save the town.

She saves the world from the scum of the universe,
As her enemies deal out the curse.

She's super strong, without a doubt,
Battling her will wear you out.

She wears indestructible bracelets which are really ace,
Because she uses them to save Earth from space.

She's a member of the Justice League,
When finishing a battle she is never fatigued.

Her real name is Princess Diana,
Her loyal subjects like fan her.

Her island is surrounded by an invisibility dome,
Just to enable her family to safely roam.

Her metal armour is as strong as a million sheets of steel,
Because of this, pain she will never feel.

She is a demi-god and she's almost immortal,
But I wish she'd disappear through a portal...
So I can rule the world!

Jack Griffin (10)
St Mary's Catholic Primary School, Fleetwood

The Emerald-Green Rage Machine

Crash! Bang! What could it be?
This creature landing, loudly on a terrifying tree.

He started off life as a minuscule and grey,
But now he's transformed and is as green as day.

In the distance, the clumsy creature tries to be in disguise,
It doesn't always work out, so often he cries.

Throughout the pitch-black darkness of night,
He tries to be calm but gives many a fright.

He likes a challenge, he likes to climb,
But be aware, he's a body full of slime.

He has an incredible mixture of brainpower and strength,
He does anything to win, he goes to great length.

The powerful, superhuman lairs in the mountainous, towering New York City,
Always a positive awe-inspiring attitude, never at all full of pity.

The emerald green Hulk, a rage machine,
He's not efficient at blending in, he's always seen.

Crash! Bang! What could it be?
The mountainous Hulk has just saved me.

Dzhuliya Hristova (10)
St Mary's Catholic Primary School, Fleetwood

The Raging Hulk

When you see the extensive Hulk,
He might be in a vast sulk,
He trains so hard to become a colossal bulk,
He is so tall, his name is the Hulk.

When he uses his car-smashing, superhuman power,
He can break the sturdiest of towers,
So he can't get in the shower,
Hulk likes to have a flower.

Massive muscles and emerald, olive skin,
He can give you a grin,
When he throws a tin,
Fifty yards into the bin!
His foe is Rhino,
When he lets out a blow,
It makes a glow,
He likes to glow.

Using his powers for hours,
He tries to get in showers,

He needs it to be as tall as towers,
His favourite flowers are sunflowers.

Although he has a lot of money,
He tries to be funny,
But he does not like curry,
Nor does he like honey.

Although he is strong,
Even though he doesn't admit he is mostly wrong,
He likes to play the gong,
And he acts like King Kong.

Ben Mellow (10)
St Mary's Catholic Primary School, Fleetwood

I Am Groot

I am suspicious and mysterious Planet X is my home,
With Rocket Racoon, I love to roam.

Me and my friends will make you groan,
But through the adventure, we will guide you home.

Make sure you grab some razor-sharp weapons,
Otherwise you'll be gone, but will need to work on.

Rocket knows my language, no one else can translate it,
Except for my friends that mend and bend the plot a bit.

Hickling up Planet X with my saw-toothed head and earthly legs,
It threads through you like no one even cares.

It's like moving into outer space.

I'm intellectual and I'm a combative tree,
But when you approach me, I will ask you what you'll do to me.

With all of my thorns, I'll jab you to death if you come near me.
When you look at me, I look scary, but I am an enhanced tree.

When Rocket helps me and the team,
We all shout with glee.

Siyana Angelova (9)
St Mary's Catholic Primary School, Fleetwood

Dark Knight

Pitch-darkness charcoal bat,
Roams the streets like a curious cat,
Glaring from his mat.

As I sit in my cop car,
I can see in front of me,
I can see afar.

Lights shimmering from downtown,
Dashing through the town
Was the malicious clown, going downtown.

I sat down, having a brew,
Then from hair-raising heights,
Landed a blue shoe.

Screams, screams, screams tower,
All because of the Joker's poisonous flower,

Flames shimmer, guns blaze,
The people of Gotham are in a gaze,
Because the guns are ablaze.

Defeating villains with a *Pow! Boom! Bash!*
It is Batman crashing down with a *smash!*

Batman's powers and might
Combined with his abilities of flight,
Glaring down with fury, as high as a kite.

Alex Gawne (11)
St Mary's Catholic Primary School, Fleetwood

Hulk Smash!

I am the Hulk, I can jump into space,
Although I can't tie a shoelace.

I once was grey but now I'm green,
That proves that I am mean.

Crash! Splash! I travel to Mars,
I definitely don't mean the chocolate bars!

"Hulk smash!" I sometimes say,
Although, I know that won't save the day.

I am as heavy as a rock,
So I can't pick a lock.

When I am travelling through space,
I like to make sure I win the race.

I rip buildings from the roots of the floor,
All because I can't fit through a door!

I adore being huge, loveable and strong,
I'm good at most things, but I can't sing a song.

I am the Hulk, I can jump to space,
Saving the world is my happy place!

Brooke Whittaker (9)
St Mary's Catholic Primary School, Fleetwood

The Terror-Striking Thor

Crash! Bang! Boom!
Thor is in the room.

As he viciously broke down the door,
It shattered to the floor.

Lightning, lightning, lightning,
Which Thor uses is frightening.

A swing of his hammer,
Could knock out a llama.

Speedily beating every villain up,
Sometimes with a plastic cup.

Thor is an awe-inspiring hero,
He's better than Emperor Nero.

Thor killed Thanos with a single strike,
With this strike, he used all his might.

As Thor travelled through space,
To Asgard, a wonderful place.

To travel to Asgard through the rainbow coloured portal,
This heroic hero will always be immortal.

Crash! Bang! Boom!
Thor is out of the room.

Blossom Martinez (10)
St Mary's Catholic Primary School, Fleetwood

Rise Of Iron Man

Boom! Sounds cover New York as he equips his enormous laserbeam,
As he runs swiftly through the town, people begin to scream.

He has some moves that can fly you to the moon,
With a click of his fingers, villains will be gone soon.

Iron Man can blast and fly, no one can beat him in the sky,
When Iron Man died in *Endgame* he said, "Bye."

His name is Tony Stark, he has some moves,
He can move faster than a horse with 1000 hooves.

He has a jetpack that can fly you to the moon,
In the afternoon, you will see him soon.

He has a base in a cave along with supercars in the stars,
His cars are faster than rocket travelling to Mars.

Alfie Southern (10)
St Mary's Catholic Primary School, Fleetwood

The Thrashing Thor

He has over ten fulfilled names,
He doesn't waste any time playing games.

With Loki as his foster brother,
They give thanks to their mother.

One green eye, one blue eye,
He has a Mjolnir,
Everyone wants one,
And so do I.

His weapon is a hammer,
He fights like he planned in in a planner.

His wife, Sif, has golden, luscious hair,
She tries to make things fair.

He has a daughter named Torunn,
She likes to hang in their hood.

He's a wall-smashing warrior,
He doesn't have a barrier.

Born 1500 years ago,
Placed in a grotto.

Demi-Doll Broughan (10)
St Mary's Catholic Primary School, Fleetwood

Marvellous Milky Way

M arvellous Milky Way everywhere you look,
A mazing photos that you took
R ed, green, yellow, blue,
V ibrant galaxies, unlike the greatest clue.
E ndless colour all around
L ooking at it as if you're proud.
L oving every moment,
O utstanding and sensational,
U nderneath the brightest glow,
S eeing the greatest show.

M aking darkness feel afraid,
I nteresting things ever made.
L oving every moment,
K eenly swirling all night long,
Y et still, never stops.

W onderful and magical,
A mazing and sensational,
Y et still never stops.

Molly Francis (10)
Werrington Primary School, Werrington

Aliens On The Moon

A bove the Earth is a beautiful sight,
L et all of the aliens shine bright.
I n the moon, aliens might live,
E very other alien could be in a sieve.
N obody has ever seen an alien, so they could be filled with light.
S ome aliens could be called Kive.

O n the moon aliens sleep,
N o aliens stay asleep.

T hese aliens might peep,
H owever, they will have fun,
E ven though they don't beep.

M oon aliens have got to stay with their mum.
O ver our heads, baby aliens meap.
O ver our heads, aliens play together,
N ow they could be eating moon cheese.

Kendal Gallacher (9)
Werrington Primary School, Werrington

Aliens Attack

A liens attack,
L istening in to demolish the world.
I nteresting for scientists,
E ndangered species of aliens, searching for blood.
N utrients we are to aliens,
S eeking for blood out of our bodies.

B eware aliens,
E ating brains for dessert.

D eadly creatures they are,
E ating us in one go.
F ierce animals,
E nding us.
A fter we're dead, throwing our bodies into lakes,
T urning, turning, can't stand the noise.
E asy to kick in the face,
D efeated aliens. *Whoo!* Yeah!

James Sherratt (9)
Werrington Primary School, Werrington

Beautiful Planets

G orgeous things so up high,
L ike a beautiful diamond in the sky.
I n the colourful sight
M ake all of the light,
M oving around the sun.
E njoy the shooting sky,
R emember, Pluto is a planet no more
I n the shinning sky.
N eptune, so far from the sun,
G etting higher and higher.

P luto, not here,
L ike it has disappeared.
A ll around so high,
N ever thinking the world is flat.
E arth, so round,
T winkling so brightly,
S aturn moves around the sun.

Miley Woodhouse (9)
Werrington Primary School, Werrington

Massive Planets

M aking space real
A nd making Earth
S afe from meteors destroying planets.
S pace planets are orbiting the sun,
I ce ring is around Saturn, so don't walk on it as it is
V ery dangerous and it will crack,
E arth is a very exciting place.

P lanets are amazing and colourful,
L ike a pretty disco ball,
A s colourful as Mars
N eptune is made out of gas, and it is the furthest away from Earth.
E arth is where we live, which is
T ruly wonderful, like the wonders of
S pace.

Marshall Miller (10)
Werrington Primary School, Werrington

Marvellous Planets

M ars has the largest volcanoes,
A nd Mars is as red as a blazing ball of fire.
R ed Planet is Mars' nickname;
V ery interesting that fact is.
E xploding amazing volcanoes everywhere.
L ovely colours sparkling everywhere.
L ook, there are lovely stars,
O ff Mars, there are lovely stars.
U ndescribable views;
S hades of red all around you.

M ercury is the closest planet to the sun,
A nd it's very gloomy.
R ockets, you need them to get there,
S tars burning bright.

Chloe Longton (9)
Werrington Primary School, Werrington

The Greatest Galaxy

G reat sights to be seen,
A nd beautiful stars shining bright,
L ight colours filling the air,
A ctually hypnotising me,
X -rays are clever, but space is better.
Y ou would love to be in this galaxy.

N othing can be better,
I t is amazing,
G reat and wonderful interesting sights,
H igh up in the sky,
T racking my eyes in the Milky Way.

S pace is beautiful,
K illing the black night sky it was before,
Y our eyes would be locked on the bright sights.

Sydney Shaw (10)
Werrington Primary School, Werrington

What Is Up In Space?

S tars, glittering like a diamond,
T winkling in the gloomy sky.
A t the top of marvellous planets
R unning out of blinding light,
S itting next to the shadowy moon.

I n the pitch-black sky,
N ot shown in the light.

T he sun is harnessing its power,
H eating up at night,
E nergy pulling throughout the stars.

S ky is dim without its light,
K icking up a ball of fire,
Y ou would have a marvellous time looking at the dazzling stars.

George Mayer (10)
Werrington Primary School, Werrington

Stars Of Space

S hining above and never stopping,
T op the light, they have like a bulb.
A ll amazed, all want to know where they go,
R ound and round the Earth, we know.
S tars are beautiful like you are.

S hining stars are amazing up high,
H ello to the astronauts up there!
I am amazed by the heartbeat of light,
N othing could be better than the night.
I n the sky, stars so bright,
N othing could top our massive light.
G o on, go to space, but don't hesitate!

Eden Leigh (9)
Werrington Primary School, Werrington

Super Star

S hooting star, you glide through the sky,
H ow magical are you?
O h, it is amazing how you fly.
O h, nobody can say shoo!
T wirl and swirl with your trail,
I ce cream, chocolate, sweets can't compare.
N obody could make a better tale.
G reat things happen when you ride through the air.

S tarting to shine bright,
T ry to wish upon a star,
A nd they make you feel light,
R ight or not, shooting star, you are best by far.

Danielle Cunningham (10)
Werrington Primary School, Werrington

The Spaceship And The Alien

S uspicious astronauts flying around in space.
P etrified in case they come across an alien.
A ll of a sudden, an alien came into sight.
C autiously, the astronaut got out of the spaceship.
E xploding galaxies got in the way of the alien.
S adly, the alien disappeared.
H orribly, the ship broke down and we had to fix it.
I ncredibly, we fixed the ship and set off again.
P ersistently, we struggled to Earth but still got there.

Kadem Mayer (10)
Werrington Primary School, Werrington

Shimmering Stars

Stars are twinkling in the air.
Shooting stars everywhere.
Sparkling bright in the sky,
Up above so high.
Stars are so dazzling they might give you a scare.

In the night sky shining,
They're bright enough to be a light.
Looking like diamonds in the sky.
You will never reach them even if try.

There are lots of stars,
They look like Mars.
Stars are created.
They look like they're naked.
Planets might come with radars.

Saphron Love (9)
Werrington Primary School, Werrington

Lunar Landings

L ots of lively stars.
U nique planets and different galaxies.
N o gravity and completely weightless.
A rrays of colour.
R oars of stars.

L unar landings are everywhere,
A nd they are high up in the air.
N o forces pulling you down.
D aring astronauts.
I ncredible lunar modules.
N o sounds to be heard.
G oing into space.
S o it was dark and plain.

Samuel Ledgar (10)
Werrington Primary School, Werrington

A Shining, Loving Star

A star that's like me,
L oving and kind.
I n fact, I can be
E njoyable and bright,
N ever gloomy like the night,
S hining bright all the time.

D ropping too much light,
A nd letting you see too much of me,
N ow this star is famous,
C reative and enormous.
I know my star is excellent,
N ext I will drop,
G oodness upon another star.

Maisy Jackson (10)
Werrington Primary School, Werrington

Spaceships

S oaring around, the colours splattered around,
P raying they are perfectly round.
A bnormally, they pick up people without a sound,
C apturing anyone in sight.
E xcellent experience of it.
S atellites can't capture them in time.
H ello, you can't say to them.
I f you see them, they're gone in the flash of an eye.
P robably won't see them in your life.

Ollie McDonnell (9)
Werrington Primary School, Werrington

Gloomy Aliens

Aliens in the sky, they are very white,
By the dazzling star so bright.
He is in love with a star,
His name is Abar.
He's extremely sneaky and never ever in sight.

   S ilent moon doesn't rise at noon.
   P lanets on fire, spitting out flames.
   A stronauts are going to shame.
   C ars can't go there or they will explode.
   E xtremely far from Earth are planets above.

Logan Parker Nixon (9)
Werrington Primary School, Werrington

Racing Rockets

Racing rockets zooming through the sky,
They take off, flying so high.
Look! Taking off! There's one.
Once they've taken off, they're gone,
If the rocket malfunctions, it won't fly.

There the huge colourful rocket goes.
Now it's no larger than my toe.
As it flies, it gets so small,
But down here it's ever so tall.
I wonder, are space creatures friend or foe?

Chloe McLoughlin (10)
Werrington Primary School, Werrington

Perfect Planets

Planets floating all around, shining so bright,
Always higher than you could fly a kite.
Perfect planets always have their days,
Always different in their own ways.
Nothing is ever out of sight.

Waves of colour floating through the air,
Colours of electricity fly through my hair.
Seven planets float through space,
Nothing is more ace.
Nobody flies to Neptune, even if they dare.

Megan Plant (10)
Werrington Primary School, Werrington

Spectacular Space

Planets, planets, big or small,
Hot or cold, and that's not all.
Comets, comets, whoosh past your face,
Shooting stars look brilliant in space.
Neptune, Uranus, Mars and Earth,
Earth is covered with sand, sea and turf.
Comets, comets, they have a head and tail,
Shooting stars leave a trail.
Pluto is the smallest planet,
It's nearly as small as a fiery comet.

Daniel Summerfield (10)
Werrington Primary School, Werrington

Planets Vs Moon!

T he magical stars light up the night
H orrific sacrifices are alright,
E ating up scraps today.

P eople going up in space,
L ightning-fast going to fly.
A ll around there's more to see,
N ever stopping the greatest peace.
E at gross food,
T o stay alive.
S peeding down as fast as light.

Flo Sawyer (10)
Werrington Primary School, Werrington

Our Galaxy

O ur galaxy is beautiful.
U nexpected shooting stars.
R otating planets around the sun.

G reat views of the stars.
A premonition of colours.
L ots of lovely colours and shining stars.
A ll the shining stars look like freezeframe fireworks.
X -ray vision is needed.
Y ou would love to see them.

Charlie Kemp (9)
Werrington Primary School, Werrington

Aliens Trying To Survive

A liens are the scariest and strange things that have ever
L ived on planets that have not been discovered.
I t is easy to breathe because they can live on Earth or in space,
E ating worms and grubs to survive.
N esting their eggs to keep them warm and safe,
S tealing stars for nightlights to keep them asleep until morning comes.

Isla Salt (10)
Werrington Primary School, Werrington

Amazing Stars And Planets

The amazing stars shining bright,
In the moonlight.
There are billions of stars,
They all have amazing art.
Planets are turning,
Whilst stars are burning.
The dazzling planets,
None of them have talents.
Stars have lots of light,
Burning in the night,
Off Mars.
There are lovely stars,
The places in the night,
And tucked up tight.

Daniella Owen (9)
Werrington Primary School, Werrington

Super Space

S tars are special
U p you go and explore
P eople that go to space
E xcited how you should feel
R ockets are used to help get to space, without them you would be lost

S tars love your heart
P lanets rotate
A ce space is where you are
C an you see us?
E mptiness is in space.

Lola Stevens (10)
Werrington Primary School, Werrington

Pleasant Planets

Planets, planets in the sky,
Like beautiful diamonds way up high.
If you love them as much as me,
They are amazing, you'll clearly see.
Spacesuit bows, you will need to tie.

Planets, planets are ever so bright,
In the dark and shiny night.
They are pretty and really nice,
One of them is as cold as ice.
Saturn is really light.

Isla Talbot (9)
Werrington Primary School, Werrington

Solar System Saturn

Saturn is always really bright.
It's hard to see in daylight.
Saturn is in the galaxy sky,
To get there, you have to fly.
When you get there, it might be night.

Saturn is very high.
All the other planets are in the sky.
Saturn has a big, icy ring;
It looks like ring finger bling.
I go in my spacesuit that I have to tie.

Maizey Statham (10)
Werrington Primary School, Werrington

Spectacular Saturn

I love Saturn,
Because of its really nice pattern,
Floating in space.
What a wonderful place!
Sixth planet from the sun,
That's a lot of fun.

I feel like I should sing.
What a wonderful ring!
Stars all around,
Looks like it's been found
Even if it's upside down,
Saturn won't frown.

Hope Clulow (10)
Werrington Primary School, Werrington

Stunning Stars And Rolling Rockets

There are lots of stars.
I can see the moon.
My rocket is failing,
There's no railing.
My engine is smoking,
And I am choking.

There's something up with my friend,
This may be the end.
I'm new here.
I'll run to the rear.
The engine made a sound.
I'm going around and around.

Charlie Edwards (10)
Werrington Primary School, Werrington

Rockets

Rockets releasing fire.
They don't have a tyre.
Wanting to see Mars,
But all they see are stars.

Rockets flying around,
Not going out of bounds.
They go by all the planets,
The rockets crashed, darn it!

Rockets are landing,
Something is banging.
It must be the moon,
I see a balloon!

Elliot Pass (9)
Werrington Primary School, Werrington

Super Saturn

S uper Saturn.
A mazing colours everywhere.
T errific ring rotating.
U nique texture.
R eally chilly.
N ice and cool.
S pecial and stunning.

R eally huge.
I ncredible and marvellous.
N ice looking.
G orgeous and great.

Violet Parton (9)
Werrington Primary School, Werrington

Alien Trouble

Aliens are coloured, they may be sea green.
They have two big eyes and have never been seen.
Sometimes they give you a frightful scare,
They can also be excitingly very rare.

They like to fly round in spaceships,
Or maybe they fly around in blips,
Maybe they are coming,
Maybe they enjoy scaring.

Millie McGill (9)
Werrington Primary School, Werrington

Stars

Stars dazzling in the sky,
Peeking down like a spy
Rising up beyond and high.

Shooting stars are like a dove,
Hovering through the sky above,
Warm enough, they don't need gloves.

Stars are gigantic balls of fire,
Rising up higher and higher,
But they will eventually expire.

Lucas Baskeyfield (10)
Werrington Primary School, Werrington

Magnificent And Perfect Planets

I see the stars.
I can't see Mars.
I see my rocket.
I look in my pocket.
What a wonderful sight,
It's so so bright!

In the night,
There's not a lot of light.
It's so slow,
I want to go!
I can't believe I'm in space,
I just really want to race.

Millie Bowker (10)
Werrington Primary School, Werrington

Out Of The Galaxies And Planets

Galaxy so bright,
All over the dark, dim, mysterious night,
Glittering like a bonfire for aliens.
It's brighter than the blinding sun that only we see,
But never in sight.

Orbiting the sun,
Looks super fun,
There's always a moon,
It wasn't too soon.

Noah Haddon (10)
Werrington Primary School, Werrington

Amazing Apollo 11

All you can see is purple and blue,
The colours are stuck together like glue.
Even though I'm in a faraway room,
I can still hear the rocket go boom.
In space, all you can hear is a pop,
Even more when you drop.
Here the rockets fly,
But it is sad to say bye.

Jacob Leach (10)
Werrington Primary School, Werrington

The Alien's Star

The galaxy floating around,
Aliens ever so round,
Aliens are green,
Could also be mean,
Stars may only weigh two pounds.

Space is all around,
Planets give off sound,
Stars are in the night sky,
There to see when we fly by,
Stars could be round.

Oliver Degg (10)
Werrington Primary School, Werrington

Numerous Worlds

Saturn is swirling.
Jupiter's twirling.
Stars were here from the beginning.
Planets are winning.
The stars are whirling.
Stars are ever so bright,
Glowing in the night.
Planets orbit around the sun,
Like a ball of fun,
Shining in the light.

Isabelle Pennington (9)
Werrington Primary School, Werrington

What Is In Space?

Up into the gloomy, dim space,
It is amazingly ace.
Planets spinning around,
Whilst looking from the ground.
The stars made a spark,
Which shone past the dark.
Up in the sky,
Where the galaxies fly,
You know, up there,
Where you stare.

Reuben Donnellan (10)
Werrington Primary School, Werrington

Outstanding Neptune

N ever explored by humans before.
E xcellent discoveries to be made.
P eculiar things to be seen.
T he dangers are high.
U nbelievably incredible.
N eptune is amazing.
E xciting new things to be found.

Isaac Williams (9)
Werrington Primary School, Werrington

Shocking Neptune

N o one has landed here before.
E very planet is older than us.
P luto is the smallest planet.
T he solar system is the best.
U ranus is very close.
N ever try to go to the sun.
E arth is near.

Sam Trowell (10)
Werrington Primary School, Werrington

Wonderful Planets

P lanets from high
L ight up the sky,
A lso, spin and orbit the sun.
N eed more to see the planets,
E xcellent view of all the planets.
T ime to take a look,
S o show me the beautiful planets.

Maddie Prince
Werrington Primary School, Werrington

Pleasant Planets And Racing Rockets

Saturn is witching.
Rockets are twitching.
Jupiter is spinning.
Planets spinning like they have a new beginning.
Rockets are zooming.
Planets are booming.
Saturn is swirling,
And a rocket is twirling.
Mars is beaming.

Ryan Wright (9)
Werrington Primary School, Werrington

The Absolutely Amazing Galaxy

Galaxy, so beautiful,
You can never imagine.
What it may bring to you,
It could be a great time.
You will travel far and wide.
Get in your spaceship and go,
Far beyond Earth
To discover
The world of space.

Olivia Edge (9)
Werrington Primary School, Werrington

Marvellous Saturn

S ome people love Saturn.
A ctually really far from here.
T oo far to reach.
U nder stars from above.
R ound the sun it goes.
N ear to Jupiter.

Grace Gilbert (9)
Werrington Primary School, Werrington

Magic Moon

Up in space with the moon it's ever so bright,
Is it day or night?
If you jump it's a big fright,
Could you fly a kite?
It might be a long flight.

Oliver Jackson (10)
Werrington Primary School, Werrington

Magical Mars

M agical Mars.
A mazing stars.
R ocketing through outer space.
S tars shooting all over the place.

Layton Mottram (10)
Werrington Primary School, Werrington

Fluffy Planet

Deep in the forest,
Too deep to know,
There's an ancient magical flower,
Submerged in the snow.

Pick off a petal,
And rub it gently,
It will make you teleport,
But don't worry, it's happened to me.

It'll take you to a planet that's unknown,
A planet that's fluffy,
A planet you won't know.

Everything is fluffy,
Yes, you heard me right,
It's a galaxy of your dreams,
You probably won't be able to sleep tonight.

There are fluffy chairs,
And fluffy games,
There are fluffy computers,
There's too much to name!

When you desire to go back home,
Then find another petal,
And rub it once more.

Maddie Byron (10)
West Walton Community Primary School, West Walton

Alien Changing

A t 12:00 there was a knock on a girl's spaceship.
L ate at night in her cosy bed, she awoke and unlocked the door.
I n shock, she found an amazing alien.
E ven though she was afraid, she stepped outside.
N on-stop playing together.

C hanging, the girl said, "I'm changing!"
H appy as can be, the girl flew,
A nd as she changed a little more she flew.
"N ever mind," said the aliens
G oing back to her spaceship she said, "Bye."
I n her spaceship, there was a mirror
N on-stop playing with the aliens
"G ot to go," she said as she flew down to Earth.

Macie Anne Maplesden (10)
West Walton Community Primary School, West Walton

The Adventure Begins

Everywhere you look, galaxies can be seen,
But one in particular, bright like a polar bear's eyes,
As I reach out to touch it,
Stardust shoots out forming a tiny figure.
Its bold eyes sparkle in the darkness of the night,
His ears prickly like a cactus,
His shiny teeth sharp as a blade.

The magnificent explosion of colour,
Fills my eyes with joy,
But then another alien shoots out making gold stars,
Disappearing out of sight.

I walk onto the galaxy,
Cautious of danger,
Suddenly something bursts out,
Letting out a roar, I've never heard before.
I run for my life and then stop,
To find myself lying in my bed next to a hideous bear!

Ellie Cavill (11)
West Walton Community Primary School, West Walton

The Big Discovery

Astronauts were in a rocket ship,
Flying for a long week when
They made a big discovery.

What they saw could not be real,
A whole new planet sitting right there
In front of their very eyes.

They came up with the name Lexwend,
But when they landed
Something else unbelievable they saw.

What they saw could not be real,
"Aliens!" they shouted
And landed as quick as they could.

When they landed, what they saw,
Aliens dancing with joy
Filling their souls with pure happiness.

So the astronauts never came back,
Instead, they partied all year long
With their new little buddies.

Maison Rider (10)
West Walton Community Primary School, West Walton

Chicken Licken

Once there was a boy,
And he liked to annoy.
So he got a chicken,
And his name was Licken.

He was very high,
Up in the sky.
So he was an alien,
And the alien was named Laylelen.

The chicken wanted to play,
So Laylelen told him to lay,
And he dropped him from the sky,
But as the chicken went, the boy said, "Bye!"

But the next day, the chicken came back,
The boy had to watch his back.
Because the chicken threw him off the sky,
And the boy knew he was going to die!

Megan Slack (11)
West Walton Community Primary School, West Walton

Space Hole

As I float through empty space and I am
Really bored, I've got no friends and
I hate floating forever
Every single day.
Another boring day has passed and I am really
Sad and lonely.
Every day I wonder if there is one
Single person out there that wants a friend.

How is that planet spinning
Oh it's a hole sucking everything is
Like a vacuum cleaner, it is
Even sucking me in, argh, help, argh.

Lyndon Barton (11)
West Walton Community Primary School, West Walton

My Asteroid

A s I venture through space and time, I
S et alight after galloping through millions of miles of nothingness.
T hen I whip myself around and head down, down and down,
E rasing everything on the planet...
R ocks, volcanoes, even mighty dinosaurs.
O ther species arrived soon after,
I nvading the old land, and
D ividing it into countries.

Arthur Buckler (10)
West Walton Community Primary School, West Walton

Steven

Hi, I am Steven.
I am an alien.
I like my friends and family, but I like invading the Earth most.
I live on the moon and enjoy it there.

One day, I decided to do what I'd always dreamed of,
I had to build a rocket ship.
I was very excited and prepared.
I set off to invade.
On the way, I saw another alien and we had a big crash!

Gracie Jane Walker (10)
West Walton Community Primary School, West Walton

Aliens Have Landed

They are ugly and all green,
The weirdest thing ever is seen.
They have an antenna on top
And their inventions are never a flop.
They hate all humans and want them gone.
They destroy our territory, like building, home or lawn.
They know how to escape when they are stranded
But for now, run, aliens have landed.

Simona Bislyte (11)
West Walton Community Primary School, West Walton

My Space Poem

S pace is up in the air. It's as cool as your dreams.
P lanets are everywhere,
A liens are around and they're scary and green.
C ome to our land where the magic happens,
E veryone loves it here, colours, stars and the moon

Norvile Petrilovskyte (10)
West Walton Community Primary School, West Walton

Floating Planets

S ometimes there are little animals floating in space,
P artly dogs and cats,
A nd there are floating foods in the sky,
C an animals float from one planet to another? Yes, they can,
E veryone can speak in space even aliens.

Samantha Blyth (10)
West Walton Community Primary School, West Walton

Planet Zog

On the planet Zog, there was a creature called Smallbird. But don't be fooled by its name, it is no ordinary bird. It has antennae, killer hearing, it plants flowers, and makes you laugh. You are happy because of Smallbird, so remember the happiness it grants you with.

Ben Notley (10)
West Walton Community Primary School, West Walton

Pluto

P luto is a planet,
L unch in space is very frantic.
U nder the stars at night,
T o the end, there is a fright.
O ops, that's just my alien friend, Spike.

Lucy Mae McClure (10)
West Walton Community Primary School, West Walton

Real Dreams

When the sun goes down,
And all sleep calm,
Something whizzes through the night.
Don't worry, it isn't a fright.
It's a dream, a real dream,
A dream in-between.
But where did it come from?
Of course, from the sea!
From the sea? How can it be?
Well, let me explain.
Water's clear and so are they.
If you'd like to see a dream, just look at a wave,
It's them swimming all day in your room at night.
What about water back from the day?
That's how fog is made,
And what, when they get to your bed?
They tell bedtime stories from inside your head.
At least, that's what I saw, or was it all a dream?

Kacper Jakub Mackowski (9)
Wood Farm Primary School, Headington

Opportunity Or Problem

Now everyone has access to the Internet,
But is it good or bad?
If you use it with proper mind,
Many good things you can find.
Here are YouTube, Facebook and WhatsApp.
The information you should pick up,
Very careful and concise,
Stop doing it otherwise.
Let's go and ask Mr Mark,
Who created Facebook,
For an answer without prank.
What he prefers, Facebook or book,
Answer will be short and exact.
He knows what causes problems in act.
Opportunities come to critical thinkers,
Who read books and Facebook avoiders.

Rukhsora Imamnazarova (11)
Wood Farm Primary School, Headington

Space Pugs

At the start of dawn,
Lots of yawns
From a few pugs
Who hated slugs.
They packed their keys,
And their cheese.
They went on a journey,
And got very dirty.
They found a van,
With a pan.
They got inside,
But one pug cried.
He needed some cheese,
But it was near bees.
They had to leave the cheese behind,
They were kind.
They put on the brake,
And baked him a cake.
They finally found their rocket,
They dug into their pockets
And found the keys.

The rocket blasted off
A pug coughed.
They looked in space,
Just in case,
And found a creature,
They called it a platypus.

Lucas Brooks (9)
Wood Farm Primary School, Headington

My Candy Dream

My name is Rosie.
I like unicorns because they're fluffy and cosy.
Once I had a dream
That I would be the queen.
Queen of the special land,
Which could only be found
When you follow your dreams
Across the candyfloss streams.

When I was riding on my horse,
A rainbow came across,
Then a funny goblin appeared with his doggy bone,
And turned my horse into a unicorn!
The land was full of sweets and treats,
And all of it was falling on the streets,
I woke up with a marshmallow pot,
Was it all a dream or not?

Klaudia Stawinska (9)
Wood Farm Primary School, Headington

Best Friend Poem

G is for grateful for everything you get.
R is for remarkable, to be extraordinary.
A is for amazing, to be me.
C is for clever, to be really good at maths.
E is for excellent, for creativity.

T is for terrific, a best friend.
H is for hilarious, making me laugh.
O is for outstanding, great in all he does.
M is for magnificent, at talking multiple languages.
A is for awesome, as awesome as can be.
S is for speedy, as speedy as a cheetah.

Grace Champion (9)
Wood Farm Primary School, Headington

Planet Zongle Bum

You should visit the planet Zongle Bum, it's very vast,
But I assure you that you'll get there rapidly fast.
On the way to the planet,
I'd recommend a pomegranate.
I felt very refreshed!

A thing or two that's important is to pay attention,
Or you'll find yourself in another dimension.
Space is very boring and empty,
But in twenty minutes you will have seen plenty.
Remember the galaxy involves legality,
So tell Zat and his crew,
That from Earth, it's you!

Ayman Saadi Mahir (9)
Wood Farm Primary School, Headington

The Galaxy A Hundred Years Ago

Sometimes I sit and wonder,
About the stuff I don't know.
Like how was the galaxy
A hundred years ago?

Did aliens fly in spaceships?
Did planets even grow?
Was Earth even here
A hundred years ago?

I wish they'd built a time machine,
And I got to go,
To see the truth about the galaxy,
A hundred years ago.

Was Pluto a planet?
Were Milky Ways filled with snow?
You can guess, but that was back
A hundred years ago!

Hamdi Guled Hasan (10)
Wood Farm Primary School, Headington

Shooting Star

S ee that flying across the sky
H igher than the moon,
O ut in space it twinkles,
O ver the clouds and moon.
T winkling like a jewel,
I t speeds through the dazzling sky,
N ot stopping for anyone,
G lowing in the glorious night.

S himmering, shooting star,
T hat shines a beaming gold
A nd glitters with a glistening glow,
R ushing in the magnificent night.

Liana Roopesh (10)
Wood Farm Primary School, Headington

The Unknown

I was led by a voice to an enchanted wood.
The creatures who live there have twinkly stars as their food.

As the sun rises, the leaves shine bright.
The pretty colours in the sky fill the forest with light.

The sunset there is even prettier than the sun rising.
If you sit on the mountain tops, the view is mesmerising.

Enchanted woods and magical mountains are amazing creations.
Then I realise the majestic land is my imagination.

Stephana Sojan (9)
Wood Farm Primary School, Headington

The Unknown Planet

I went to Westgate and walked into a shop.
It took me to a shopping space planet.
I had realised that I was the first one there.
My wallet was so heavy.
I bought many things, I could.
But suddenly, I couldn't find a way out...
Wait, I had seen a button
Which had a sign saying *Earth.*
I pushed it and found myself in my room,
On my cosy bed, and my shopping in my drawers.
So I asked myself,
Should I tell anyone?

Inaaya Bibi Asghar (11)
Wood Farm Primary School, Headington

The New Appearance Of Life Gone Wrong

Neil Armstrong being watched by millions on TV.
He saw something freaky and walked closer so he could see.
He could almost guarantee it was as big as a tree.
He didn't think it was a plea to see something so creepy.
The creature was very squeaky.
It was coming near Neil Armstrong step by step,
But he didn't notice because it was very sneaky.
It came and took Neil very speedily,
So next time, make sure your eyes are beady.

Daniella Drizi (9)
Wood Farm Primary School, Headington

The Seasons

Autumn is when puddles
Are here and there,
And when golden leaves,
Fall everywhere.

Winter invites snow and
Frost to play,
And gets tired easily,
So there are shorter days.

Spring settles in and
Renews life again,
Animals come to play,
Like cows and hens.

In summer, there is
Never a dull day,
Children laugh in the
Sun, ready to play.

Adina Nadeem-Aftab (10)
Wood Farm Primary School, Headington

My Voice

My voice is a bit quiet.
My voice is loud when I shout my heart out.
My voice is quiet when I whisper in places.
My voice begins at the bottom of the deep blue trench.
My voice will be bursting out of a megaphone.
My voice will speak up for climate change.
My voice will stop pollution.
My voice will save lives.
My voice will stop wars.
But my voice is just amazing.

Manroop Singh (10)
Wood Farm Primary School, Headington

White

White can be the colour of clouds, floating across the sky.
White is the colour of snowdrops which are the first flowers to appear in spring.
White is the colour of snow, the messenger of winter.
White is the colour of polar bears, who live in the freezing lands of the Arctic.
White can be the colour of a swan, who is graceful and elegant.

Senara Bambaravanage (11)
Wood Farm Primary School, Headington

Sparkly Fireworks

Midnight is the time
To sparkle
With joy,
With red, orange, blue, green,
Taste fine, like me.
Pop! Bang! Whoosh!
Me and my friends squeal,
What should be in the forest is in the sky!
We are shimmering in reflective light,
If I know you will know me,
So think carefully.

Hadia Haydari (10)
Wood Farm Primary School, Headington

Aliens

A liens are radioactive green.
L ively aliens play blobball on the ring of Saturn.
I n outer space, aliens float around.
E dward the alien is a good magician.
N ear Saturn is Uranus, with aqua blue aliens.
S urely aliens will be discovered some day?

Harry Stillman
Wood Farm Primary School, Headington

Strong

S uper strength
T o destroy the
R ebel side.
O n top of the world.
N ot a coward.
G ood at everything.

Almuez Amier Alagab (11)
Wood Farm Primary School, Headington

YOUNG WRITERS INFORMATION

We hope you have enjoyed reading this book – and that you will continue to in the coming years.

If you're a young writer who enjoys reading and creative writing, or the parent of an enthusiastic poet or story writer, do visit our website www.youngwriters.co.uk. Here you will find free competitions, workshops and games, as well as recommended reads, a poetry glossary and our blog. There's lots to keep budding writers motivated to write!

If you would like to order further copies of this book, or any of our other titles, then please give us a call or order via your online account.

Young Writers
Remus House
Coltsfoot Drive
Peterborough
PE2 9BF
(01733) 890066
info@youngwriters.co.uk

Join in the conversation!
Tips, news, giveaways and much more!

YoungWritersUK   @YoungWritersCW